Unbelievable Pictures and Facts About Rhode Island

By: Olivia Greenwood

Introduction

Rhodes is a very special place filled with lots of history. It is a very popular tourist destination. Today we will be exploring Rhodes in more detail.

Where in the world is Rhodes situated?

Far away in Athens on the southeastern side lies Rhodes. Rhodes is the biggest island in the Greek Dodecanese group. It is situated in the country of Greece.

Is Rhodes an old place?

Rhodes dates back to many years ago. There is a long history associated with Rhodes. Although we don't know exactly how old Rhodes is, we do know that in 1912 Italy seized Rhodes.

Are there any legends about Rhodes?

There are many legends associated with Rhodes. One such legend talks about Rhode who was a protector of Rhodes and the seas. She fell in love with Helios who was the sun god and they got married.

Who is believed to be the first founder of Rhodes?

Believe it or not, there is a very old legend about Rhodes. Many people believe that the very first founder of Rhodes was none other than Hercules himself.

How many people currently reside in Rhodes?

There are currently on average just over a million people who stay in Rhodes.

What type of weather do they experience in Rhodes?

The climate in Rhodes is a Mediterranean climate. The summer months are very warm and humid, while the winter months are pretty cold and rainy.

What is the landscape in Rhodes like?

Rhodes has a very fascinating landscape. It is surrounded by mountains, beaches, and cliffs.

Which languages do they speak in Rhodes?

In Rhodes people speak different languages. The most common language which is spoken in Rhodes is English. Some of the other languages spoken consist of Arabic, Korean and Mandarin.

What type of financial currency do they use in Rhodes?

Due to the fact that Rhodes is a part of the European Union, it makes use of the same currency as the rest of Europe. The financial currency which is used in Rhodes in the euro.

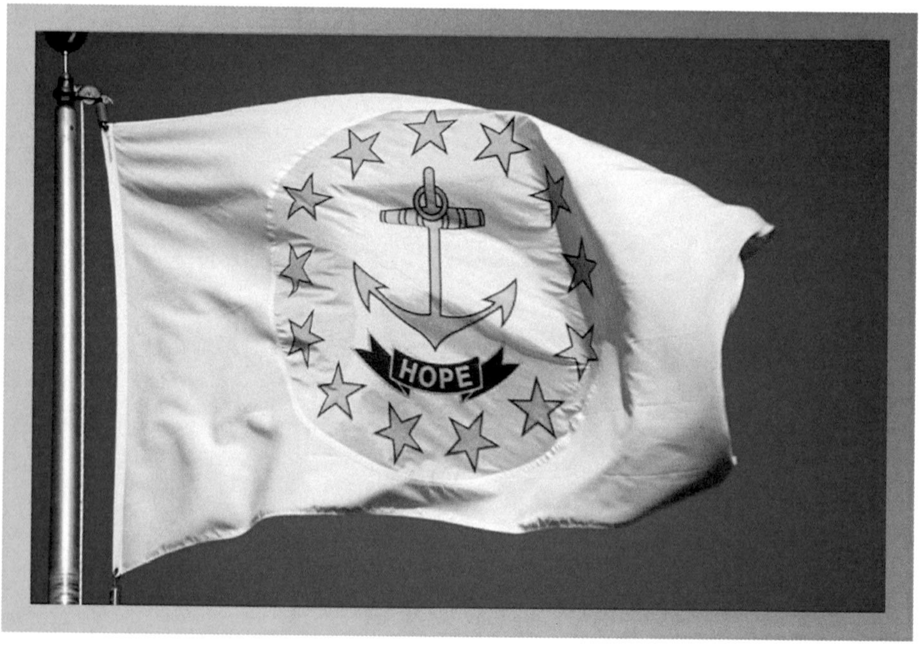
HOPE

Is there a symbol that represents Rhodes?

The answer is yes. There is a very special and unique breed of deer which is the official symbol of Rhodes.

What does the name Rhodes translate to?

If you directly translate the name of Rhodes, you will end up with the word rose. Rose is a very good description of Rhodes as the area has many beautiful flowers including roses.

Does Rhodes have a nickname?

There are a few nicknames which have been given to Rhodes over the years. The one nickname worth mentioning is Emerald city.

Has Rhodes always had the same name?

Throughout the years Rhodes has had a variety of different names. It was called Snake Island at one point. At another point, it was called Star Island.

What makes the area well-known?

Rhodes is well known to everyone throughout the world. The reason for this fame is because of the statue which was known as the Colossus of Rhodes.

Was there a famous monument in the area?

Yes, the Colossus of Rhodes was a very famous statue. It was the highest statue that existed. This famous statue was of the Greek god Helios. Unfortunately, an earthquake destroyed it. However, it remained for 56 years.

Are there any ancient tourist attractions?

There are a couple of great tourist attractions in Rhodes. One of the most famous tourist attractions worth mentioning is the Acropolis of Lindos. This magnificent site is an ancient archeological site.

Are there different sectors in Rhodes?

There are different sectors in Rhodes. The one area which is a huge tourist attraction is the Medieval town of Rhodes. This forms a part of the Old Rhodes and is filled with tons of history, old buildings, and atmosphere.

What type of foods do people eat in Rhodes?

People eat all sorts of different foods in Rhodes. They eat a special handmade type of pasta with cheese and butter. This dish is known as Matsi or plasta. They also eat a dish called Psaria marinata which is a delicious pickled fish dish. There are tons of interesting and fascinating foods to discover and taste in Rhodes.

Have there been any important laws in Rhodes?

Back in the days, the first comers to Rhodes came up with a code of conduct and laws for the sea. These laws were named the Rhodian Law. They are still the basis used for the laws of the sea today.

Is Rhodes a popular tourist attraction?

The answer is yes, Rhodes is a popular tourist destination. On average over a million people come to visit Rhodes each and every single year. The history of Rhodes is what makes Rhodes so popular.

Made in the USA
Monee, IL
25 April 2022

95385969R00026